# SO YOU WANT TO BE AN ASTRONAUT

Written by **Clayton Anderson**

Illustrated by **Iris Amaya**

PUBLISHED BY SLEEPING BEAR PRESS™

# So, you want to be

# an ASTRONAUT?

It is a job that's super cool.
   To ultimately become one, you must work quite hard in school.
   It's not a job that's easy, you'll need many skills to conquer space,
      But if you read through this great book, in no time you'll be an ace!

The skill set of an astronaut combines so many things.
You might fix toilets or be on TV, whatever that day brings.
It's not easy to work and live in space, but man, will it be fun.
So, buckle up. Enjoy the ride. Your training has begun!

**Teamwork** is a skill we need in everything we do.

And astronauts will use it too when working with their crew.

On our mission there will be those times when we're not sure what comes next.

So, we'll compromise, cooperate, and achieve some great success!

You can practice teamwork daily; it does not matter where you are.
Just help a friend or share a task—you'll be a teamwork star.
If you see someone who looks in need, always lend a helping hand.
For when you work together, the results will be so grand!

Each day will bring us challenges when we're working up in space.

But completion of the task at hand will put a smile into place.

**Working hard while staying calm**—traits like these will guide our way.

If we finish strong, with nothing wrong, then we'll get some time to play!

To practice this can be quite hard but will bring great satisfaction.

You can be so proud you did your best in every move and action.

It seems to me this never fails to result in time well spent

Then you'll follow up tomorrow, with that same focus and intent.

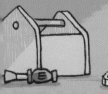

**Listening** seems so simple, as the ears hear what folks say.

But it's a very special skill you must practice every day.

Good listeners know that listening is more than the words you hear.

You must focus on what's being said. You want the message to be clear.

Astronauts must listen carefully to the ground if we're in trouble.
If we force them to repeat their words, the time lost can more than double.
Good response to space emergencies needs our actions quick and sure,
And if we do things right to start, then our ship will be secure.

When Mom or Dad say, "please clean your room," you might just pout or frown.
But keeping track of all your stuff should never get you down.
If you are not careful, your backpack fills . . . and becomes a huge black hole!
But **being organized** can make you feel you're always in control.

In orbit there is quite a need to know where all things are.
Less gravity can be a pain, as things will float soooo far.
To be a top-notch astronaut, I will share a needed trait:
Be organized and know what's where. Then life in space is great!

Working hard in outer space can bring stress to the mind.
We need to find some clever ways to help ourselves unwind.
For astronauts in orbit, there are several things to do,
I loved to look out windows and search for places like Katmandu!

Life on Earth can be just as tough, so you'll need to find a way,
To calm your thoughts, gain focus, and get back into your day.
A perfect way to **manage stress** is to read a book like this,
Or take a walk, play with a friend; whatever brings you bliss.

**Working fast creatively** is a skill all astronauts show.
We must be thinking on our feet and letting answers flow.
Finding clever solutions to the many problems at hand,
Helps us survive while up in space when something goes unplanned.

So brainstorm lots ... learn all you can. Be active in your school.
   The things you know and understand are what gives your brain its fuel.
When a problem rears its ugly head, you'll know where to find the fix.
   Your brain will be up to the task—filled with facts and nifty tricks.

No matter the situation, astronauts must always speak the truth.
(This is something we have all been taught, since early in our youth.)
So many folks are counting on the things we do and say,
That we must reflect true honesty in every single way.

The same applies for everyone who lives down here on the Earth.
Your **truthfulness and honesty** are reflections of your worth.
It isn't hard to speak the truth, but sometimes it takes nerves,
To summon up the courage that the truth most certainly deserves.

Flying jets and doing space walks means astronauts must be fit,
If we're not **healthy** fliers, then the mission could take a hit.
So exercising every day is a big part of our plan.
In orbit, miles up in space, it consumes a two-hour span.

So move however you enjoy! That will keep your body sound.
Run or dance or climb a tree. Jump or swim, just horse around!
Listen to your body. Feed it well and grow up strong.
And you'll be ready for outer space—the place where you belong.

**Being kind and using manners** is something NASA will demand.
So astronauts must treat folks right—from coworkers to fans.
They say kindness doesn't cost a thing—and space fliers know it's true.
We listen first and remember always, to say "please" and then "thank you."

You too can be like astronauts, by showing that you're kind.
It's simple and not hard to do—shouldn't even cross your mind.
Use empathy, be generous. Have concern for one another.
Practice with your friends and classmates—even try it with your brother.

Some say that astronauts are brave, and I imagine this is true.
But equally important is, you must believe in YOU.
By working hard and training smart, we will be so well prepared
That there won't be any time in space we will ever think we're scared.

So while working toward a spaceflight—or another dream—it's key
To focus all your efforts and be as prepared as you can be.
While bravery is the trait we seek, to get there take this cue:
Preparation is what shows your team you have **confidence** in YOU!

Whether you dream to be an astronaut, or pursue a different goal,
Make it something that's the best of you, a career that makes you whole.
You don't have to be a genius—you'll just need a solid base,
The time is now, begin your quest. Step to it, start the chase!

# So, you want to be

# an ASTRONAUT?

—now you know just what it takes.
Practice these skills, full steam ahead, and don't ever hit the brakes.
It's not a job for everyone, but it's one you can embrace.
Stay true to you, work hard, and smile...

# I'll see you up in SPACE!

# Astronaut and Cosmonaut FUN FACTS!

## What important skills and traits from the book do you see here?

**YURI GAGARIN**, a Russian cosmonaut, was the first human to reach outer space. He achieved this remarkable feat in 1961, just months before the first American, Alan B. Shepard, would do it.

**JOHN GLENN** was the oldest American male astronaut to fly in space at age 77 and the first American to orbit our Earth. Sally Ride was the youngest American female, reaching orbit at age 32, until Hayley Arceneaux—a private citizen and cancer survivor—flew on the SpaceX Inspiration 4 crew in 2021. She was just 29 years old at the time.

**DR. MAE C. JEMISON** was the first African American woman to travel into space. An engineer and physician, she did so on space shuttle *Endeavour* flight STS-47 in 1992, spending nearly eight days in orbit.

The first space walk ever performed by an American was by astronaut **ED H. WHITE II**. He spent about 36 minutes outside of his Gemini 4 spacecraft on June 3, 1965, performing the first EVA (extra-vehicular activity) in United States history. Space walks today can last more than eight hours!

**LELAND MELVIN** played college football at Richmond University and was drafted by the NFL's Detroit Lions! His first flight was aboard the space shuttle *Atlantis* on STS-122 in 2008. His Lions jersey is on display at the Pro Football Hall of Fame in Canton, Ohio.

**CLAYTON ANDERSON** is the only astronaut to have ever refereed a Division I Men's College basketball game.

Astronaut **MIKE MASSIMINO** had a recurring role on the TV comedy show "*The Big Bang Theory*," playing an astronaut who flies to the International Space Station with the show's MIT engineering character Howard Wolowitz (call sign Fruit Loops!).

**NICOLE STOTT** was the first to paint a watercolor image of the beautiful Caribbean Sea while living on the International Space Station. Karen Nyberg did quilting in space!

**CHRIS HADFIELD**, a Canadian astronaut, made a recording of David Bowie's song "Space Oddity," singing about fictional astronaut Major Tom, while living aboard the International Space Station.

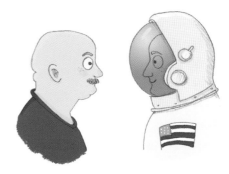

The **KELLY BROTHERS, SCOTT AND MARK**, were the first pair of twins to become astronauts! Both flew into space multiple times, with Scott spending nearly a year in orbit on the space station. Before that flight, they became subjects for a key NASA science "twins" experiment, evaluating how the human body behaves on Earth (Mark) and in space (Scott).

**FRANK CULBERTSON** was the only American in space on September 11, 2001. He captured a famous photograph of the Twin Towers in New York City after the attack.

**SUNITA WILLIAMS**, or "Suni" as she is better known, was famous for her dog Gorby—a Jack Russell terrier—whose cardboard image made many appearances with famous people from around the world. She also ran the Boston Marathon on the space station treadmill at the very same time as those running it in Boston on the ground!

To my family...
and those who dare to lead.
Be yourself always and let the chips fall where they may.
And to Audrey, Sarah, Julia and my friends at Sleeping Bear Press...
thank you for believing.

—Clayton

✳

To my son and all his friends.
Hopefully this book will help you to travel and explore new galaxies.

—Iris

SLEEPING BEAR PRESS™
2395 South Huron Parkway, Suite 200
Ann Arbor, MI 48104
www.sleepingbearpress.com

Printed and bound in the United States.

10 9 8 7 6 5 4 3 2 1

Library of Congress Cataloging-in-Publication Data

Names: Anderson, Clayton C., 1959- author. | Amaya, Iris, illustrator.
Title: So you want to be an astronaut / written by Clayton Anderson ;
illustrated by Iris Amaya.
Description: Ann Arbor, MI : Sleeping Bear Press, [2023] | Audience: Ages 6-10. |
Summary: In rhyming text, looks at the ways aspiring astronauts can
prepare for blast-off. Includes fun facts about astronauts and cosmonauts.
Identifiers: LCCN 2023017952 | ISBN 9781534111851 (hardcover)
Subjects: CYAC: Stories in rhyme. | Astronauts—Fiction. | Ability—Fiction.
| LCGFT: Stories in rhyme. | Picture books.
Classification: LCC PZ8.3.A5446 So 2023 | DDC [E]—dc23
LC record available at https://lccn.loc.gov/2023017952